# Recovei

# Addictions

## Dale & Juanita Ryan

*6 Studies for* ·
*Groups or Individuals*

With Notes for Leaders

◤ *LIFE RECOVERY GUIDES*

INTERVARSITY PRESS
DOWNERS GROVE, ILLINOIS 60515

*InterVarsity Press is the book-publishing division of InterVarsity Christian Fellowship, a student movement active on campus at hundreds of universities, colleges and schools of nursing in the United States of America, and a member movement of the International Fellowship of Evangelical Students. For information about local and regional activities, write Public Relations Dept., InterVarsity Christian Fellowship, 6400 Schroeder Rd., P.O. Box 7895, Madison, WI 53707-7895.*

*All Scripture quotations, unless otherwise indicated, are from the Holy Bible, New International Version. Copyright © 1973, 1978, International Bible Society. Used by permission of Zondervan Bible Publishers.*

*Cover illustration: Tim Nyberg*

*ISBN 0-8308-1155-9*

*Printed in the United States of America*

| 12 | 11 | 10 | 9 | 8 | 7 | 6 | 5 | 4 | 3 |
|----|----|----|---|---|---|---|---|---|---|
| 99 | 98 | 97 | 96 | 95 | 94 | 93 | 92 | 91 | |

# An Invitation to Recovery

Life Recovery Guides are rooted in four basic convictions.

First, we are in need of recovery. The word *recovery* implies that something has gone wrong. Things are not as they should be. We have sinned. We have been sinned against. We are entangled, stuck, bogged down, bound and broken. We need to be healed.

Second, recovery is a commitment to change. Because of this, recovery is a demanding process and often a lengthy one. There are no quick fixes in recovery. It means facing the truth about ourselves, even when that truth is painful. It means giving up our old destructive patterns and learning new life-giving patterns. Recovery means taking responsibility for our lives. It is not easy. It is sometimes painful. And it will take time.

Third, recovery is possible. No matter how hopeless it may seem, no matter how deeply we have been wounded by life or how often we have failed, recovery is possible. Our primary basis for hope in the process of recovery is that God is able to do things which we cannot do ourselves. Recovery is possible because God has committed himself to us.

Finally, these studies are rooted in the conviction that the Bible can be a significant resource for recovery. Many people who have lived through difficult life experiences have had bits of the Bible thrown at their pain as a quick fix or a simplistic solution. As a result, many people expect the Bible to be a barrier to recovery rather than a resource. These studies are based on the belief that the Bible is not a book of quick fixes and simplistic solutions. It is, on the contrary, a practical and helpful resource for recovery.

We were deeply moved personally by these biblical texts as we worked on this series. We are convinced that the God of the Bible can bring serenity to people whose lives have become unmanageable. If you are looking for resources to help you in your recovery, we invite you to study the Bible with an open mind and heart.

### Getting the Most from Life Recovery Guides

Life Recovery Guides are designed to assist you to find out for yourself what the Bible has to say about different aspects of recovery. The texts you will study will be thought-provoking, challenging, inspiring and very personal. It will become obvious that these studies are not designed merely to convince you of the truthfulness of some idea. Rather, they are designed to allow biblical truths to renew your heart and mind.

We want to encourage realistic expectations of these discussion guides. First, they are not intended to be everything-the-Bible-says about any subject. They are not intended to be a systematic presentation of biblical theology.

Second, we want to emphasize that these guides are not intended to provide a recovery program or to be a substitute for professional counseling. If you are in a counseling relationship or are involved in a support group, we pray that these studies will enrich that resource. If you are not in a counseling relationship and your recovery involves long-term issues, we encourage you to consider seeking the assistance of a mental health professional.

What these guides are designed to do is to help you study a series of biblical texts which relate to the process of recovery. Our hope is that they will allow you to discover the Good News for people who are struggling to recover.

There are six studies in each Life Recovery Guide. This should provide you with maximum flexibility in how you use these guides. Combining the guides in various ways will allow you to adapt them to your time schedule and to focus on the concerns most important to you or your group.

All of the studies in this series use a workbook format. Space is provided for writing answers to each question. This is ideal for personal study and allows group members to prepare in advance for the discussion. The guides also contain leader's notes with suggestions on how to lead a group discussion. The notes provide additional background information on certain questions, give helpful tips on group dynamics and suggest ways to deal with problems that may arise during the discussion. These features enable someone with little or no experience to lead an effective discussion.

## Suggestions for Individual Study

**1.** As you begin each study, pray that God would bring healing and recovery to you through his Word.

**2.** After spending time in personal reflection, read and reread the passage to be studied.

**3.** Write your answers in the spaces provided or in a personal journal. Writing can bring clarity and deeper understanding of yourself and of the Bible. For the same reason, we suggest that you write out your prayers at the end of each study.

**4.** Use the leader's notes at the back of the guide to gain additional insight and information.

**5.** Share what you are learning with someone you trust. Recovery is empowered by experiences of community.

## Suggestions for Group Study

Even if you have already done these studies individually, we strongly encourage you to find some way to do them with a group of other people as well. Although each person's recovery is different, everyone's recovery is empowered by the mutual support and encouragement that can only be found in a one-on-one or a group setting. Several reminders may be helpful for participants in a group study:

**1.** Realize that trust grows over time. If opening up in a group setting is risky, realize that you do not have to share more than what feels safe to you. However, taking risks is a necessary part of recovery. So, do participate in the discussion as much as you are able.

**2.** Be sensitive to the other members of the group. Listen attentively when they talk. You will learn from their insights. If you can, link what you say to the comments of others so the group stays on the topic. Also, be affirming whenever you can. This will encourage some of the more hesitant members of the group to participate.

**3.** Be careful not to dominate the discussion. We are sometimes so eager to share what we have learned that we do not leave opportunity for others to respond. By all means participate! But allow others to do so as well.

**4.** Expect God to teach you through the passage being discussed and through the other members of the group. Pray that you will have a profitable time together.

**5.** We recommend that groups follow a few basic guidelines, and that these guidelines be read at the beginning of each discussion session. The guidelines, which you may wish to adapt to your situation, are:

    a. Anything said in the group is considered confidential and will not be discussed outside the group unless specific permission is given to do so.

    b. We will provide time for each person present to talk if he or she feels comfortable doing so.

    c. We will talk about ourselves and our own situations, avoiding conversation about other people.

    d. We will listen attentively to each other.

    e. We will be very cautious about giving advice.

    f. We will pray for each other.

If you are the discussion leader, you will find additional suggestions and helpful ideas for each study in the leader's notes. These are found at the back of the guide.

# Recovering from Addictions

Addictions have always been a part of the human predicament. Addictions of one kind or another have always enslaved people. They have always led to spiritual, emotional, social and, sometimes, physical death.

Addiction can be defined as the habitual use of a substance or the habitual practice of a behavior to control one's mood in spite of the fact that the substance or the behavior creates repeated problems. Chemicals, food, people, sex, work, spending, gambling and religious practices are a few of the things that can become addictive. We can become addicted to any substance or behavior which alters our mood, or which anesthetizes us to our emotional pain. It is not just the alcoholics on skid row that have a problem with addiction! Keith Miller describes the extent of the problem in this way:

Sometime people—especially religious people—do not realize that when they use things like food, work, cigarettes, or tranquilizers to "quiet their nerves" they are keeping themselves from facing the anxieties and denial in their lives as much as if they were drowning them in alcohol. . . . The excessive use of tranquilizers and sleeping pills, excessive smoking, drinking, working, religious work, and addictions to excitement, to sex, and to people (including our children)—all these things are crippling "normal people" daily. The startling fact is that, because of denial, we only see the destructive nature of these things clearly in the lives of other people. We minimize our own compulsive and addictive behaviors and honestly believe that we don't have a problem.[1]

Gerald May provides a helpful list of the characteristics of addiction. He says that when we are addicted, the first sign is tolerance. We require increased quantities of a substance or increased frequency of a behavior to provide the same mood alteration. A second characteristic is withdrawal. We find it very uncomfortable if we are not able to continue our addiction. Self-deception, the third characteristic of addiction, comes as we minimize or deny the problems which our addictions create. The fourth characteristic is loss of willpower. We find ourselves unable to freely choose to stop. Finally, there is a distortion of attention, as we become idolatrously attached to the addictive substance or behavior.[2]

Recovery from addictions is a spiritual journey. The Twelve Steps of Alcoholics Anonymous recognize the spiritual nature of recovery, and they have, consequently, been a vital resource to hundreds of thousands of people seeking recovery from addictions.[3] We want to encourage you, if you have not already done so, to join a fellowship of people who are using the Twelve Steps as a guide for their recovery from addiction.

The six studies in this Life Recovery Guide are based on the structure of the first three steps of Alcoholics Anonymous. The Twelve Steps are based on biblical principles and reflect the wisdom gained from many years of experience in recovery. We are convinced that the Bible is a rich storehouse of hope and healing for people struggling with addictions. Our prayer is that these studies will help to guide, sustain and enrich your recovery.

*May your roots sink deeply in the soil of God's love.*

*Dale and Juanita Ryan*

---

[1]Keith Miller, *Sin: The Ultimate Deadly Addiction* (San Francisco: Harper and Row, 1987), pp. 77-78.

[2]Gerald G. May, *Addiction and Grace* (San Francisco: Harper and Row, 1988), pp. 26-31.

[3]See Leader's Notes for a complete list of the Twelve Steps of Alcoholics Anonymous.

# 1
# Admitting
# Our
# Powerlessness

*"I can handle it. I learned a long time ago that no one else is going to take care of me. I need to be strong enough to take care of myself, otherwise I will not survive."*

The journey from reliance on our own power to an admission of powerlessness is often a very long and very difficult one. We do not easily abandon the myths of power and control. Our very survival seems to depend on these myths. Letting go of them seems to be full of risk and danger.

Facing the reality of our powerlessness is, however, the first step in recovery from addictions. It is a step which takes courage. And, it is a necessary step. As long as we stay in denial, believing that we are able to take care of our own needs and to solve our problems by our own efforts, we will shut God out of our lives. There is no way to receive help and healing until our myths of power are surrendered.

Sometimes the chaos created by our addictions forces us to see clearly our need for help. Sometimes the people who care about us will lovingly tell us the truth about who we have become, giving us an opportunity to break out of our denial. However it happens, recovery begins when our myth of power comes to an end.

Somehow God's power breaks through our denial and illuminates our powerlessness. What has become obvious to everyone else, becomes obvious to us. We can't manage by ourselves. We can no longer control our lives. We are powerless over our addictions. We need help. This terrible, painful recognition is where recovery begins.

☐ **Personal Reflection** _____

**1.** What makes it difficult for you to face the reality that you are not powerful enough to handle your problems alone?

**2.** What events in your life have helped you to face the reality of your powerlessness over your addiction?

**3.** What does "powerlessness" mean to you?

☐ **Bible Study**————————————————————

As Jesus went on from there, he saw a man named Matthew sitting at the tax collector's booth. "Follow me," he told him, and Matthew got up and followed him.

While Jesus was having dinner at Matthew's house, many tax collectors and "sinners" came and ate with him and his disciples. When the Pharisees saw this, they asked his disciples, "Why does your teacher eat with tax collectors and 'sinners'?"

On hearing this, Jesus said, "It is not the healthy who need a doctor, but the sick. But go and learn what this means: 'I desire mercy, not sacrifice.' For I have not come to call the righteous, but sinners." (Matthew 9:9-13)

**1.** What insights did you gain during your time of personal reflection?

**2.** The Pharisees were religious leaders who avoided contact with "sinners" in an attempt to please God. It is reasonable to assume that the Pharisees would identify people with addictions as sinners to be avoided and rejected. What effect does religiously justified rejection have on people struggling with addiction?

**3.** What do you think Matthew the tax collector needed—instead of rejection—from the religious community?

**4.** Jesus said, "It is not the healthy who need a doctor but the sick." What is the point Jesus is making with this metaphor?

**5.** Jesus said, "I have not come to call the righteous, but sinners." What are the dangers of being "righteous"?

**6.** What motivates us to hang on to our false sense of righteousness and to our sense of power over our own lives?

**7.** Jesus also said, "Go and learn what this means: 'I desire mercy, not sacrifice.' " What does this mean?

**8.** How could learning to be merciful to yourself and others help you to face your powerlessness over your addiction?

☐ **Personal Reflection** ———————————————————

What would you like to say to the God who understands that you are powerless over your addiction?

# 2
# Admitting Our Lives Are Unmanageable

> *"I've worked hard to keep things under control. But the harder I try, the more out-of-control things seem to get. I'm sick and tired of being sick and tired."*

In the early stages of the addictive process, the use of addictive chemicals and addictive behaviors can help us to sustain the illusion that we are in charge. Each fix confirms the illusion that things aren't so bad.

Eventually, however, the "fix" stops working. Life becomes completely unmanageable. We see the price tag for our addiction go up and up. Our health and relationships deteriorate. But we find ourselves continuing to pursue our addiction no matter what the price. At this stage it seems that the harder we try to control our behavior, the more out-of-control we become.

We hang on as long as possible to the myth that we can manage. One day, however, the nightmare of our lives catches up with us. We see that, in spite of all our attempts at control, we are out of control. We see that, in spite of all our efforts to manage, our lives have become unmanageable.

This is part of the first step toward healing and recovery. We will need to return again and again to this most basic truth: we are powerless over our addiction, and our lives have become unmanageable.

☐ **Personal Reflection** ————————————————————

**1.** What does it mean to you that your life is unmanageable?

**2.** What thoughts and feelings do you have about yourself in response to the sense of being out-of-control?

☐ **Bible Study**————————————————————————

We know that the law is spiritual; but I am unspiritual, sold as a slave to sin. I do not understand what I do. For what I want to do I do not do, but what I hate I do. And if I do what I do not want to do, I agree that the law is good. As it is, it is no longer I myself who do it, but it is sin living in me. I know that nothing good lives in me, that is, in my sinful nature. For I have the desire to do what is good, but I cannot carry it out. For what I do is not the good I want to do; no, the evil I do not want to do—this I keep on doing.

Now if I do what I do not want to do, it is no longer I who do it, but it is sin living in me that does it.

So I find this law at work: When I want to do good, evil is right there with me. For in my inner being I delight in God's law; but I see another law at work in the members of my body, waging war against the law of my mind and making me a prisoner of the law of sin at work within my members. What a wretched man I am! Who will rescue me from this body of death? Thanks be to God—through Jesus Christ our Lord!

So then, I myself in my mind am a slave to God's law, but in the sinful nature a slave to the law of sin.

Therefore, there is now no condemnation for those who are in Christ Jesus, because through Christ Jesus the law of the Spirit of life set me free from the law of sin and death. (Romans 7:14—8:2)

---

**1.** What insights did you gain during your time of personal reflection?

**2.** How does Paul describe the unmanageability of his life?

**3.** Paul says that he does not have the ability to simply choose to do what he knows to be right. How does this compare with your experience?

4. What makes this admission so difficult for us?

5. Why is it important to admit that we have lost control and that our lives have become unmanageable?

6. Paul asks, "Who will rescue me?" Then he breaks into praise: "Thanks be to God through Jesus Christ our Lord!" What do you think led Paul to express thankfulness in this way?

7. The practical focus of God's power in this text is to free us from

condemnation. In what ways do you condemn yourself?

**8.** Meditate for a few minutes on the following: Picture the behaviors that have made your life unmanageable. Allow yourself to experience the fear and sadness that these addictive behaviors create, especially the fear of how God will respond to you. Now, picture Jesus saying: "I know about these behaviors, I know how unmanageable your life has become. I do not condemn you." Let yourself experience the surprise and the hope which these words bring.

What thoughts or feelings do you have in response to this meditation?

☐ **Prayer** _____

What would you like to say to the God who does not condemn you even when your life is unmanageable?

# 3
# Believing God's Power Is Greater

*"I knew I couldn't make it on my own. My life had become insane. But, I resisted God. In the first place, I didn't know if he really was powerful. But, more importantly, I was afraid that, if he was powerful, he would use his power to punish me."*

The foundations of the Christian faith rest on the conviction that God is more powerful than we are. God is powerful enough to help and heal us. He is powerful enough to restore sanity to our chaotic lives. He is the Mighty God, Creator of heaven and earth.

Coming to believe in God's power is not a simple step for people who struggle with addictions because we have spent so much energy trying to convince ourselves that we are powerful. We have insisted on our own competence. We are the managers of our own lives. We have played god for so long that we have grown to like the part. Once we have recognized the unmanageability of our lives, however, we can begin to let go of our impossible expectations of ourselves and to let God be God.

There are further complications to believing in God's power for people who struggle with addictions. Many of us may believe that

God is powerful but vengeful, spiteful, irrational and eager to punish. Because of these very negative ideas about God, coming to believe in God's power can be full of terror. The key to this step of recovery lies in coming to believe that God's power is a power "for us" rather than "against us." The issue is not just whether or not God is powerful in some abstract theological sense, but whether God's power is shaped by compassion and mercy, or shaped by vindictiveness.

The Bible is clear about God's power. He is the Mighty God. But, he is also "God with us." His power is life-giving, not death-giving. God longs to use his power to lift us from the hell of addictions into the serenity of his presence.

□ **Personal Reflection** _____

**1.** What did you learn as a child about God's power?

**2.** What do you believe about God's power at this point in your recovery?

□ **Bible Study** _____

Hear, O LORD, and answer me,
    for I am poor and needy.

Guard my life, for I am devoted to you.
    You are my God; save your servant
    who trusts in you.
Have mercy on me, O Lord,
    for I call to you all day long.
Bring joy to your servant,
    for to you, O Lord,
    I lift up my soul.
You are forgiving and good, O Lord,
    abounding in love to all who call to you.
Hear my prayer, O LORD;
    listen to my cry for mercy.
In the day of my trouble I will call to you,
    for you will answer me.

I will praise you, O Lord my God, with all my heart;
    I will glorify your name forever.
For great is your love toward me;
    you have delivered me from the depths of the grave.

The arrogant are attacking me, O God;
    a band of ruthless men seeks my life—
    men without regard for you.
But you, O LORD, are a compassionate and gracious God,
    slow to anger, abounding in love and faithfulness.
Turn to me and have mercy on me;
    grant your strength to your servant
    and save the son of your maidservant.
Give me a sign of your goodness,
    that my enemies may see it and be put to shame,
    for you, O LORD, have helped me and comforted me.
        (Psalm 86:1-7, 12-17)

**1.** What insights did you gain during your time of personal reflection?

**2.** What does the writer say about God's power?

**3.** People trapped in addictions often think of God as powerful, but believe that his power is punitive. In contrast, the author describes God as one whose power is for us, not against us. What does he say about God's character which could help you to see that his power is for you?

**4.** People trapped in addictions may also believe that God's power is unavailable to them. In contrast, the writer testifies that God has been helpful to him in powerful ways. What does he say God has done for him?

**5.** What makes it difficult for you to believe that God is both powerful and interested in helping you?

**6.** What has God done for you in the past that might help you to believe that he is both powerful and interested in helping you?

**7.** The writer asks God to act powerfully on his behalf. He asks God to guard his life, have mercy on him, bring him joy, teach him his way, grant him strength and give him a sign of his goodness. How do you need God to act powerfully on your behalf?

**8.** If, as the writer suggests, God is powerful, compassionate and interested in helping you, how could this help you in your recovery from addiction?

☐ **Prayer** _____

What do you need to receive from the God who is more powerful than you?

# 4
# Being Restored

*"I knew I had a problem. But insanity is such a strong word. I know now that I was working so hard to deny reality, to find ways to blame others and to make excuses that I was unable to think clearly or to behave rationally."*

Addictions lead to insanity. Becoming insane involves losing the ability to think clearly and to behave rationally. Terence Gorski uses the metaphor of target shooting to talk about the insanity of addiction.

Sanity has a reasonable sequence and order to it, a kind of "ready, aim, fire." The insanity which comes from addictions is more like "ready, fire, blow off your foot, aim, and blame somebody else!"[1]

People do "crazy" things in order to continue their addictions. When a substance or behavior becomes the god of a person's life, insanity eventually results.

Emotional insanity might range from anesthetized emotions to out-of-control hysteria. Social insanity might be demonstrated by blaming, abusing or abandoning people who don't help you continue your addiction. Cognitive insanity comes from the twisted, distorted thinking that addicted people use to "make sense" out of their behavior. And, of course, the fundamental insanity is the continuation of the addictive behavior in spite of the multiple problems it creates.

The restoration of sanity requires a power significantly greater than our own. We need a God who is genuinely powerful, interested in our restoration and compassionate toward us. The second step of the healing process invites us to believe in this kind of God. The biblical text for this study records the story of a man who found God to be both more powerful than himself and able to restore him to sanity.

## ☐ Personal Reflection ————————————————————————————

**1.** What about your life in the past or the present has been insane?

**2.** How is your life different, or how would your life be different if God's power restored you to sanity?

## ☐ Bible Study————————————————————————————

"O king, be pleased to accept my advice: Renounce your sins by doing what is right, and your wickedness by being kind to the oppressed. It may be that then your prosperity will continue."

Twelve months later, as the king was walking on the roof of the royal palace of Babylon, he said, "Is not this the great Babylon I have built as the royal residence, by my mighty power and for the glory of my majesty?"

The words were still on his lips when a voice came from heaven, "This is what is decreed for you, King Nebuchadnezzar: Your royal authority has been taken from you. You will be driven away from people and will live with the wild animals; you will eat grass like cattle. Seven times will pass by for you until you acknowledge that the Most High is sovereign over the kingdoms of men and gives them to anyone he wishes."

Immediately what had been said about Nebuchadnezzar was fulfilled. He was driven away from people and ate grass like cattle. His body was drenched with the dew of heaven until his hair grew like the feathers of an eagle and his nails like the claws of a bird.

At the end of that time, I, Nebuchadnezzar, raised my eyes toward heaven, and my sanity was restored. Than I praised the Most High; I honored and glorified him who lives forever. (Daniel 4:27; 29-34)

---

**1.** What insights did you gain during your time of personal reflection?

**2.** Daniel is the speaker at the beginning of this passage. He advises the King to change his behavior and to be kind to the oppressed.

Who is it that experiences oppression as a result of addiction?

**3.** The King did not listen to this advice. What are the dangers inherent in the way the King did respond?

**4.** What is the consequence of the King's response?

**5.** The King testifies, "I, Nebuchadnezzar, raised my eyes to heaven and my sanity was restored." What does it mean to raise our eyes to heaven?

**6.** What is the relationship between raising our eyes to heaven and the restoring of sanity to our lives?

**7.** Reflect on the ways in which God has restored you to sanity. Take a few minutes to write a short prayer to God thanking him or asking him to restore you to sanity.

☐ **Prayer** ————————————————————————

What do you need to receive from the God who is able to restore you to sanity?

---

[1]Terence T. Gorski, *Passages through Recovery* (San Francisco: Harper and Row, 1989), pp. 29-30.

# 5
# Turning Our Wills Over to God

*"It is terrifying for me to think about turning my will over to God. I've learned not to trust anyone, not even God. But, I have also learned that my will-power isn't a higher power. I know I need help. I know I need to turn my will over to someone more powerful than myself."*

Admitting our powerlessness and the unmanageability of our lives and coming to believe that God is powerful enough to restore us to sanity are the foundations on which recovery is built. But admitting certain things and coming to believe other things is not all there is to recovery.

Recovery demands that we make a critical decision: Will we continue to make the kinds of choices which have led to insanity or will we surrender our wills to God's care? The choice we face in recovery is between continuing to make insane decisions and beginning to turn our wills over to God's care.

But, can God be trusted with my will? Does he really care about me? Given the insanity my life has become, why should God want anything to do with me? These questions are part of the struggle of recovery. It will take courage to trust God. But, trusting God doesn't have to be done in monthly installments. It can only be done, in fact, one day at a time.

☐ **Personal Reflection** _____

**1.** What fears do you experience as you consider turning your will over to God?

**2.** What motivates you to want to do this, in spite of your fears?

☐ **Bible Study** _____

Now what I am commanding you today is not too difficult for you or beyond your reach. It is not up in heaven, so that you have to ask, "Who will ascend into heaven to get it and proclaim it to us so we may obey it?" Nor is it beyond the sea, so that you have to ask, "Who will cross the sea to get it and proclaim it to us so we may obey it?" No, the word is very near you; it is in your mouth and in your heart so you may obey it.

See, I set before you today life and prosperity, death and destruction. For I command you today to love the LORD your God, to walk in his ways, and to keep his commands, decrees and laws; then you will live and increase, and the LORD your God will bless you in the land you are entering to possess.

But if your heart turns away and you are not obedient, and if you are drawn away to bow down to other gods and worship them, I declare to you this day that you will certainly be destroyed. You will not live long in the land you are crossing the Jordan to enter and possess.

This day I call heaven and earth as witnesses against you that I have set before you life and death, blessings and curses. Now choose life, so that you and your children may live and that you may love the LORD your God, listen to his voice, and hold fast to him. (Deuteronomy 30:11-20)

---

**1.** What insights did you gain during your time of personal reflection?

**2.** The text presents two options. We can choose life and prosperity, or we can choose death and destruction. How are addictions a way of choosing death and destruction?

**3.** How can recovery from addictions lead to life?

**4.** This text says that choosing life is not too difficult or beyond our reach. What is it about addictions that can make choosing life seem beyond our reach?

**5.** What gives you hope that recovery is not beyond your reach?

**6.** The text suggests that choosing life is possible because "The word [of God] is very near you; it is in your mouth and in your heart so you may obey it." Turning our wills over to the care of God is not a violation of who we are. It is a fulfillment of our deepest desires.

How has this been true in your own recovery?

7. God is not a disinterested observer of our choices. He wants us to choose life. He says, "Now choose life." How might this help you decide to turn your will over to the care of God?

8. Making the decision to choose life is not a one-time event, but a one-day-at-a-time event. Reflect for a moment on what the choice of death would look like for you today.

Now reflect on what the choice of life would look like for you today. Listen to God say to you, "Choose life." Picture yourself listening to his voice, staying close to him and turning over your will to his care.

What were your thoughts and feelings during this reflection?

## ☐ Prayer

What would you like to say to the God who can be trusted to care for your will?

# 6
# Turning Our Lives Over to God

*"I was prepared to consider turning my addiction over to God but I didn't want it to go any further than that. I think I wanted God to take away my alcoholism so that I could keep on drinking. I wanted God to remove my problems and the pain in my life so I could manage my life better."*

Many people approach the third step prepared to consider turning over to God the parts of their life which are causing them the most trouble. Unfortunately, no part of life is insulated from our addictions.

We need to turn our thinking over to God because we are confused. We need to turn our emotions over to God because we don't know what to do with emotional pain—except to anesthetize ourselves. We need to turn our shame over to God because shame feeds our desires to continue in the addiction. We need to turn our hopes and dreams over to God because our distorted thinking tends to idealize the future.

Our problems are not a just a minor footnote to a life which is basically running smoothly. The problem is with all of life. All of it needs to be turned over to God.

We begin by surrendering as much as we can to God. It is important in this process that we stay honest about our fears, doubts and hesitations. At first we may only be able to ask God to help us want to surrender to him. God accepts us where we are. He will help us to surrender, little by little, day by day, to his loving care.

As with the other steps, this is not a do-it-now-and-get-it-over-with proposition. It is a step that we come back to every day. And with each new decision to surrender to God's care, our trust will grow.

## ☐ Personal Reflection ————————————————

**1.** What has helped you to trust God to care for you?

**2.** What experiences have you had as you have turned your life over to God's care?

## ☐ Bible Study———————————————————

Therefore, I urge you, brothers in view of God's mercy, to offer your bodies as living sacrifices, holy and pleasing to God—this is your spiritual act of worship. Do not conform any longer to the pattern of this world, but be transformed by the renewing of your mind. Then you will be able to test and approve what God's will is—his good, pleasing and perfect will. (Romans 12:1-2)

**1.** What insights did you gain during your time of personal reflection?

**2.** Paul urges us to turn our lives over to God because of God's mercy. How does seeing God as being merciful help in the struggle to turn our lives over to his care?

**3.** When Paul urges us to offer our bodies as "living sacrifices to God," he is urging us to turn our lives over to God. At this stage in your recovery what does it mean for you to turn your life over to God?

**4.** In what ways have you been able to do this?

**5.** Paul urges us to "not be conformed to the pattern of this world." What specific patterns do you see yourself needing to ask God to help you change?

**6.** This biblical text calls us to be transformed by the renewing of our minds. What renewing of perspectives, values and beliefs have you experienced that have contributed to your recovery?

**7.** A transformation is an ongoing process of change. In addition to breaking the cycle of addiction, what transformations or changes have you experienced during your recovery?

8. The text says that God's will for us is "good, pleasing and perfect." God's desires for us are for good not for evil. What evidence have you seen of this truth in your life?

☐ **Prayer** ————————————————————————————

What would you like to say to the God who can be trusted to care for your life?

# Leader's Notes

You may be experiencing a variety of feelings as you anticipate leading a group using a Life Recovery Guide. You may feel inadequate and afraid of what will happen. If this is the case, know you are in good company. Many of the kings, prophets and apostles in the Bible felt inadequate and afraid. Many other small group leaders share the experience of fear as well.

Your willingness to lead, however, is a gift to the other group members. It might help if you tell them about your feelings and ask them to pray for you. Keep in mind that the other group members share the responsibility for the group. And realize that it is God's work to bring insight, comfort, healing and recovery to group members. Your role is simply to provide guidance for the discussion. The suggestions listed below will help you to provide that guidance.

### Using the Life Recovery Guide Series

This Life Recovery Guide is one in a series of eight guides. The series was designed to be a flexible tool that can be used in various combinations by individuals and groups—such as support groups, Bible studies and Sunday-school classes. Each guide contains six studies. If all eight guides are used, they can provide a year-long curriculum series. Or if the guides are used in pairs, they can provide studies for a quarter (twelve weeks).

We want to emphasize that all of the guides in this series are designed to be useful to anyone. Each guide has a specific focus, but all are written with a general audience in mind. Additionally, the workbook format allows for personal interaction with biblical truths, making the guides adaptable to each individual's unique journey in recovery.

The four guides which all individuals and groups should find they can most easily relate to are *Recovery from Distorted Images of God, Recovery from Loss, Recovery from Bitterness* and *Recovery from Shame.* All of us need to replace our distorted images of God with biblically accurate images. All of us experience losses, disappointments and disillusionment in life, as well as loss through death or illness. We all have life experiences and relationships which lead to bitterness and which make forgiveness difficult. And we all experience shame and its debilitating consequences.

The four other guides are *Recovery from Codependency, Recovery from Family Dysfunctions, Recovery from Abuse* and *Recovery from Addictions.* Although these guides have a more specific focus, they address issues of very general concern both within the Christian community and in our culture as a whole. The biblical resources will be helpful to your recovery even if you do not share the specific concerns which these guides address.

Individuals who are working on a specific life issue and groups with a shared focus may want to begin with the guide which relates most directly to their concerns. Survivors of abuse, for example, may want to work through *Recovery from Abuse* and follow it with *Recovery from Shame.* Adult children from dysfunctional families may want to begin with *Recovery from Family Dysfunctions* and then use *Recovery from Distorted Images of God.* And those who struggle with addictive patterns may want to begin with *Recovery from Addictions* and then use *Recovery from Codependency.*

There are many other possibilities for study combinations. The short descriptions of each guide on the last page, as well as the information on the back of each guide will help you to further decide which guides will be most helpful to your recovery.

## Preparing to Lead

**1.** Develop realistic expectations of yourself as a small group leader. Do not feel that you have to "have it all together." Rather, commit yourself to an ongoing discipline of honesty about your own needs. As you grow in honesty about your own needs, you will grow as well in your capacity for compassion, gentleness and patience with yourself and with others. As a leader, you can encourage an atmosphere of honesty by being honest about yourself.

**2.** Pray. Pray for yourself and your own recovery. Pray for the group members. Invite the Holy Spirit to be present as you prepare and as you meet.

**3.** Read the study several times.

**4.** Take your time to thoughtfully work through each question, writing out your answers.

**5.** After completing your personal study, read through the leader's notes for the study you are leading. These notes are designed to help you in several ways. First, they tell you the purpose the authors had in mind while writing the study. Take time to think through how the questions work together to accomplish that purpose. Second, the notes provide you with additional background information or comments on some of the questions. This information can be useful if people have difficulty understanding or answering a question. Third, the leader's notes can alert you to potential problems you may encounter during the study.

**6.** If you wish to remind yourself during the group discussion of anything mentioned in the leader's notes, make a note to yourself below that question in your study guide.

## Leading the Study

**1.** Begin on time. You may want to open in prayer, or have a group member do so.

**2.** Be sure everyone has a study guide. Decide as a group if you want people to do the study on their own ahead of time. If your time together is limited, it will be helpful for people to prepare in advance.

**3.** At the beginning of your first time together, explain that these studies are meant to be discussions, not lectures. Encourage the members of the group to participate. However, do not put pressure on those who may be hesitant to speak during the first few sessions. Clearly state that people do not need to share anything they do not feel safe sharing. Remind people that it will take time to trust each other.

**4.** Read aloud the group guidelines listed in the front of the guide. These commitments are important in creating a safe place for people to talk and trust and feel.

**5.** The covers of the Life Recovery Guides are designed to incorporate both symbols of the past and hope for the future. During your first meeting, allow the group to describe what they see in the cover and respond to it.

**6.** Read aloud the introductory paragraphs at the beginning of the discussion for the day. This will orient the group to the passage being studied.

**7.** The personal reflection questions are designed to help group members focus on some aspect of their experience. Hopefully, they will help group members to be more aware of the frame of reference and life experience which they bring to the study. The personal reflection section can be done prior to the group meeting or as the first part of the meeting. If the group does not prepare in advance, approximately ten minutes will be needed for individuals to consider these questions.

The personal reflection questions are not designed to be used directly for group discussion. Rather, the first question in the Bible study section is intended to give group members an opportunity to reveal what they feel safe sharing from their time of personal reflection.

**8.** Read the passage aloud. You may choose to do this yourself, or prior to the study you might ask someone else to read.

**9.** As you begin to ask the questions in the guide, keep several things in mind. First, the questions are designed to be used just as they are written. If you wish, you may simply read them aloud to the group. Or you may prefer to express them in your own words. However, unnecessary rewording of the questions is not recommended.

Second, the questions are intended to guide the group toward understanding and applying the main idea of the study. You will find the purpose of each study described in the leader's notes. You should try to understand how the study questions and the biblical text work together to lead the group in that direction.

There may be times when it is appropriate to deviate from the study guide. For example, a question may have already been answered. If so, move on to the next question. Or someone may raise an important question not covered in the guide. Take time to discuss it! The important thing is to use discretion. There may be many routes you can travel to reach the goal of the study. But the easiest route is usually the one we have suggested.

**10.** Don't be afraid of silence. People need time to think about the question before formulating their answers.

**11.** Draw out a variety of responses from the group. Ask, "Who else has some thoughts about this?" or "How did some of the rest of you respond?" until several people have given answers to the question.

**12.** Acknowledge all contributions. Try to be affirming whenever possible. Never reject an answer. If it seems clearly wrong to you, ask, "Which part of the text led you to that conclusion?" or "What do the rest of you think?"

**13.** Realize that not every answer will be addressed to you, even though this will probably happen at first. As group members become more at ease, they will begin to interact more effectively with each other. This is a sign of a healthy discussion.

**14.** Don't be afraid of controversy. It can be very stimulating. Differences can enrich our lives. If you don't resolve an issue completely, don't be frustrated. Move on and keep it in mind for later. A subsequent study may resolve the problem. Or, the issue may not be resolved—not all questions have answers!

**15.** Stick to the passage under consideration. It should be the source for answering the questions. Discourage the group from unnecessary cross-referencing. Likewise, stick to the subject and avoid going off on tangents.

**16.** Periodically summarize what the group has said about the topic. This helps to draw together the various ideas mentioned and gives continuity to the study. But be careful not to use summary statements as an opportunity to give a sermon!

**17.** During the discussion, feel free to share your own responses. Your honesty about your own recovery can set a tone for the group to feel safe in sharing. Be careful not to dominate the time, but do allow time for your own needs as a group member.

**18.** Each study ends with a time for prayer. There are several ways to handle this time in a group. The person who leads each study could lead the group in a prayer or you could allow time for group participation. Remember that some members of your group may feel uncomfortable about participating in public prayer. It might be helpful to discuss this with the group during your first meeting and to reach some agreement about how to proceed.

**19.** Realize that trust in a group grows over time. During the first couple meetings, people will be assessing how safe they will feel in the group. Do not be discouraged if people share only superficially at first. The level of trust will grow slowly but steadily.

### Listening to Emotional Pain

Life Recovery Guides are designed to take seriously the pain and struggle that is part of life. People will experience a variety of emotions during these studies. Your role as group leader is not to act as a professional counselor. Instead it is to be a friend who listens to emotional pain. Listening is a gift you can give to hurting people. For many, it is not an easy gift to give. The following suggestions can help you listen more effectively to people in emotional pain.

**1.** Remember that you are not responsible to take the pain away. People in helping relationships often feel that they are being asked to make the other person feel better. This is usually related to the helper's own patterns of not being comfortable with painful feelings.

**2.** Not only are you not responsible to take the pain away, one of the things people need most is an opportunity to face and to experience the pain in their lives. They have usually spent years denying their pain and running from it. Healing can come when we are able to face our pain in the presence of someone who cares about us. Rather than trying to take the pain away, commit yourself to listening attentively as it is expressed.

**3.** Realize that some group members may not feel comfortable with expressions of sadness or anger. You may want to acknowledge that such emotions are uncomfortable, but remind the group that part of recovery is to learn to feel and to allow others to feel.

**4.** Be very cautious about giving answers and advice. Advice and answers may make you feel better or feel competent, but they may also minimize people's problems and their painful feelings. Simple solutions rarely work, and they can easily communicate "You should be better now" or "You shouldn't really be talking about this."

**5.** Be sure to communicate direct affirmation any time people talk about their painful emotions. It takes courage to talk about our pain because it creates anxiety for us. It is a great gift to be trusted by those who are struggling.

## The Twelve Steps of Alcoholics Anonymous[1]

1. We admitted we were powerless over alcohol—that our lives had become unmanageable.

2. Came to believe that a Power greater than ourselves could restore us to sanity.

3. Made a decision to turn our will and our lives over to the care of God as we understood Him.

4. Made a searching and fearless moral inventory of ourselves.

5. Admitted to God, to ourselves, and to another human being the exact nature of our wrongs.

6. Were entirely ready to have God remove all these defects of character.

7. Humbly asked Him to remove our shortcomings.

8. Made a list of all persons we had harmed, and became willing to make amends to them all.

9. Made direct amends to such people wherever possible, except when to do so would injure them or others.

10. Continued to take personal inventory and when we were wrong promptly admitted it.

11. Sought through prayer and meditation to improve our conscious contact with God as we understood Him, praying only for knowledge of His will for us and the power to carry that out.

12. Having had a spiritual awakening as the result of these steps, we tried to carry this message to alcoholics, and to practice these principles in all our affairs.

The following notes refer to the Bible study portion of each study:

### Study 1. Admitting Our Powerlessness. Matthew 9:9-13.

*Purpose:* To understand our need for help from God.

**Question 2.** For people who are addicted, rejection increases shame, increases the desire to escape into addiction, strengthens the denial system and leaves no hope for recovery. The Pharisees' attitude toward "sinners" is very similar to the moralistic rejection of alcoholics and other addicted people that occurs today. Persons who are addicted are seen as bad people, as sinners. Until we get beyond this sort of simpleminded moralizing, we cannot expect to understand the heart of Jesus or the needs of addicted people.

**Question 3.** Matthew needed acceptance and valuing instead of judgment from people who saw themselves as morally superior. Being accepted and valued is critical to recovery from addictions.

**Question 4.** Notice that Jesus uses a disease metaphor for the human predicament. We are ill. We need a physician. We have a cancer that we cannot cure by ourselves.

The point is that denial keeps us from getting the help we need. If we have a cancerous lump on our neck, but ignore it and pretend we are healthy, we will die of cancer. If we pretend that we are healthy spiritually, that we can somehow be religious enough or good enough on our own, we will ignore our need for God and live in separation from him.

**Question 5.** The sort of "righteousness" which Jesus rejects here is a smug self-powered holiness. The pharisaic mentality includes the conviction that I can control my life and achieve holiness through my own efforts; I am a powerful person because I can do all these things. Jesus rejected this kind of power religion in favor of a religion that is rooted in our admission of powerlessness. The righteousness Jesus is concerned with here is a self-reliant righteousness that is full of denial and pretense. It is a righteousness that separates us from God and allows us to feel capable of judging others. If we pretend to be able to handle our problems with addiction on our own, it will continue to control and destroy us.

**Question 6.** We do this because (1) we have been taught that we need to work hard to please God; (2) it makes us feel more capable and in control; (3) it keeps us from having to face the truth about our limits and failures; and 4) it is very difficult for us to trust that God is loving and merciful toward us. We would rather trust ourselves to somehow make it on our own than to trust God's love.

**Question 7.** "Sacrifice" refers to religious behaviors. Jesus is saying that God does not want us to try to prove ourselves to him, to ourselves or to others by performing religious practices. Attempts at religious perfectionism separate us from an awareness of our need for God and separate us from other people. We become more concerned with our religious success than we are with people and their needs. This can lead to the kind of religious abuse of others that characterized the Pharisees in this story. What God does want is for us to be merciful. Mercy requires that we see our own need. From that perspective we can see the need of others.

**Question 8.** As we experience God's deep compassion for us when we are troubled and weak, we can begin to accept ourselves as he does. We can begin to have the courage to let go of our denial and face the truth about our powerlessness to help ourselves. We can be gentle and forgiving of ourselves as we struggle with the first step of recovery. As we let go of our denial and practice mercy toward ourselves, we will become more merciful toward others. We will let go of blaming them for our problems. We will see their trouble and weakness and find ourselves growing in compassion for them.

### Study 2. Admitting Our Lives Are Unmanageable. Romans 7:14—8:2.

*Purpose:* To see that our lives are unmanageable but that God does not condemn us.

**Question 2.** Paul is confused. He says, "I don't understand what I do." He describes his experience as an inner war between the part of him that "delights in God's law" and the part of him that is "a prisoner of the law of sin." He focuses on the dilemma that his will does not seem to control his actions.

The disconnection between will and behavior is characteristic of addictions and compulsions. Early in the addictive process people may choose the addictive substance, but later in the process people find that, even though they desperately want to stop their addictive behavior, their wills are no longer empowered to make this choice.

**Question 4.** We all want to believe that we are in control of our lives, that we can choose our behavior. It is terrifying to realize: I am out of control. In addition to the general difficulty of admitting that life is unmanageable, which is shared by all addicted people, Christians who are addicted face unique difficulties. We are accustomed to understanding faith as a matter of decision. If our ability to decide is damaged by the addictive process, we may be terrified that we will be condemned.

**Question 5.** This admission allows us to step out of denial and to face the reality of our addictions and the chaos they are creating. We have to face this painful reality in order to begin our recovery.

**Question 6.** The transitions from confession ("What a wretched man I am!"), to longing for rescue ("Who will rescue?"), to praise ("Thanks be to God") are complex. Several points should be noted: (1) For many people the word *wretched* is closely connected with a spirituality that suggests that the worse you feel about yourself, the more likely God is to approve of you. God never asks us to punish ourselves, hate ourselves or verbally abuse ourselves. Paul's expression of wretchedness is an expression of his desperation and his feelings of powerlessness. (2) Paul becomes acutely aware of his need for help. (3) He remembers God. He remembers God's love. He remembers that God does not condemn him. He remembers God's provision of help through Jesus.

**Question 8.** If shame and condemnation could cure our addictions, we would all be better by now. Just the opposite is true. Shame and condemnation are the soil in which addictions grow. People caught in addictions and compulsions come to believe that there is no hope. The only escape seems to be to continue with the addiction because the addiction numbs these feelings of self-condemnation and hopelessness. This text says that in spite of the fact that I cannot freely choose to do what is right, God does not condemn me.

**Study 3. Believing God's Power Is Greater. Psalm 86:1-7, 12-17.**
*Purpose:* To realize that God's power is greater than ours and that his power is for us, not against us.

**Question 2.** The author understands the unique power of God. He says there is no one like God. No actions can compare with God's.

**Question 3.** He says that God is forgiving, good and abounding in love to all who call on him. He is compassionate, gracious, slow to anger, abounding in love and faithfulness. Encourage the group to focus on these qualities and their significance.

**Question 4.** The writer says that God will answer him in the day of his trouble, that he has delivered him from the depths of the grave and that he has helped and comforted him. Encourage group members to focus on these actions of God and how they are needed by a person struggling with addictions.

**Question 7.** Addictions confuse us. We don't know what we need. If we had divine power on call to use as we wish, we would probably use it to continue our addictions. God's power, however, is a power for healing, not for destruction. We can expect that God will be powerfully present to guard our life and bring us joy, but we cannot expect that God will be available to help us continue our destructive addictions.

**Question 8.** These truths about God provide the basis for the hope and courage we need in the recovery process. We have seen that we are not powerful enough to help ourselves. The reality that there is a Higher Power who is powerful and loving and ready to help us will allow us to continue to let go of our denial and will give us the strength to ask for help.

### Study 4. Being Restored. Daniel 4:27, 29-34.

*Purpose:* To see that God can restore our sanity.

**Question 2.** To oppress is to crush or burden spiritually or mentally. Addictions crush the person who is addicted as well as the family members and close friends of the person who is addicted. One person's addiction oppresses many people.

**Question 3.** The text does not mention any immediate response by the king. We find a year later, however, that the king's arrogance continues to feed his denial. He is confident of his great and self-sufficient power. From his point of view, there is no reason why someone as powerful as he is should change his behavior. The king sees himself as a god. He does not know his limits. He has no awareness that what he has is a gift from the true God. The denial and arrogance lead him to false security and to heartless oppression of others.

**Question 4.** Notice that the voice from heaven states what will happen to the King as a simple matter of fact, not as a threat of punishment. It is the King's choice that brings the results. And the consequences are quite dramatic. The king loses his power and ends up living in the wild like an animal. His insane thinking led him to insane behavior.

**Question 5.** This was an admission by Nebuchadnezzar that he was not the most powerful one. He is saying: "There is a heaven above me. There is a power greater than I. I am not God. I am willing to acknowledge that God is God." It is a first step out of denial toward surrender.

**Question 6.** Understanding that we are creatures is one of the foundations of sanity. People who cease to "raise their eyes toward heaven" replace God with something, often making their addictions gods. Addicted people give to mood altering substances or behaviors that which rightly belongs to God. Raising our eyes to heaven is an act of faith in a power greater than ourselves who is able to restore us to sanity.

**Study 5. Turning Our Wills Over to God. Deuteronomy 30:11-20.**
*Purpose:* To see that God can be trusted with the choices and decisions of life.

**Question 2.** Addictions bring emotional, social and spiritual death. Some addictions also cause physical death.

**Question 3.** Recovery is the process of restoring emotional, physical, relational and spiritual health. It is important to remember, however, that addicted people often have grandiose images about what life without addictions will be like. The goal of recovery is not to achieve a life of euphoria, but to live a sober, serene life. Sobriety and the first stages of recovery will actually cause us to experience more pain, not less, because the numbing effect of our addiction is removed. Recovery leads to life, but the road is not an easy one.

**Question 4.** Addictions are very powerful forces. If we could just stop them, we would. If our ability to make healthy choices is damaged, how can we make good choices? People who are struggling with addictions often either overestimate their abilities to control their addiction: "I can stop whenever I want; there's no problem." Or, they underestimate the possibilities for recovery: "I can't do anything to stop; there's no hope." Both of these extremes feed the addictive cycle. Recovery is not easy. But it can be done.

**Question 5.** The point of these verses is not a simple-minded, you-can-do-it optimism. Hope in this text and hope in recovery come from the conviction that God is actively involved in the process. It is not beyond reach because, even when I have no power, there is a power higher than my own.

**Question 6.** People who are addicted have lost touch with their heart's desire. Their lives are consumed by the next fix as if it is all that matters in life. Recovery allows persons to rediscover the true desires of their hearts—their true values, dreams and longings. Addictions destroy life and love. Recovery restores both.

**Question 7.** God is on our side in recovery. He does not want our wills in order to use them against us. He is our Creator, our Compassionate Father, our Friend. He longs for us to live with him in peace and joy and blessing.

**Study 6. Turning Our Lives Over to God. Romans 12:1-2.**
*Purpose:* To understand our need to turn all of life over to the care of God.

**Question 2.** Addicted people often expect to be judged without mercy. The expectation of judgment grows out of our distorted image of God and out of experiences of judgment from others. It would be impossible for us to genuinely turn our lives over to the care of someone whom we expect to be unmerciful. But the Bible consistently teaches that God is merciful. He is tender, forgiving and compassionate. In view of his mercy, we can trust him to truly care for us.

**Question 5.** Recovery from addiction always takes place in a hostile environment. Recovering alcoholics will be exposed to literally thousands of commercials and advertisements which suggest that a connection exists between alcohol and the good life. People struggling with anorexia may be complimented on their weight loss. Workaholics may experience the rewards of being very "successful." The pattern of this world is the pattern of denial. Encourage group participants to explore the ways in which their recovery requires them to find different patterns for living.

**Question 6.** Addictions lead to frozen feelings, dishonesty, secrets, isolation, judgmentalism, perfectionism, moral compromises, self-centeredness, the illusion of control and confused mental processes. The goal of recovery is not just to stop using a mood-altering substance or behavior, but rather to experience a renewing of our minds. The renewal of our minds in recovery includes (1) a new honesty about ourselves, (2) a new valuing of relationships, (3) a new valuing of our feelings, (4) a new acceptance of ourselves and of others, and (5) a new ability to reach out to others to help and be helped.

**Question 7.** The changes experienced in recovery are many. We learn to break our isolation and begin to spend time with others in recovery. We begin to be appropriately responsible for meeting our obligations. We begin to make amends. We begin to talk about our thoughts and feelings. We learn to listen to others.

---

[1]The Twelve Steps are taken from *Alcoholics Anonymous,* 3rd ed. (New York: A. A. World Services Inc.), pp. 59-60. Reprinted with permission.

*For more information about Christian resources for people in recovery and subscription information for* STEPS, *the newsletter of the National Association for Christian Recovery, we invite you to write to:*

*The National Association for Christian Recovery*
*P.O. Box 11095*
*Whittier, California 90603*

## LIFE RECOVERY GUIDES FROM INTER-VARSITY PRESS
*By Dale and Juanita Ryan*

*Recovery from Abuse.* Does the nightmare of abuse ever end? After emotional, verbal and/ or physical abuse how can you develop secure relationships? Recovery is difficult but possible. This guide will help you turn to God as you put the broken pieces of your life back together again. Six studies, 64 pages, 1158-3.

*Recovery from Addictions.* Addictions have always been part of the human predicament. Chemicals, food, people, sex, work, spending, gambling, religious practices and more can enslave us. This guide will help you find the wholeness and restoration that God offers to those who are struggling with addictions. Six studies, 64 pages, 1155-9.

*Recovery from Bitterness.* Sometimes forgiveness gets blocked, stuck, restrained and entangled. We find our hearts turning toward bitterness and revenge. Our inability to forgive can make us feel like spiritual failures. This guide will help us find the strength to change bitterness into forgiveness. Six studies, 64 pages, 1154-0.

*Recovery from Codependency.* The fear, anger and helplessness people feel when someone they love is addicted can lead to desperate attempts to take care of, or control, the loved one. Both the addicted person's behavior and the frenzied codependent behavior progress in a destructive downward spiral of denial and blame. This guide will help you to let go of over-responsibility and entrust the people you love to God. Six studies, 64 pages, 1156-7.

*Recovery from Distorted Images of God.* In a world of sin and hate it is difficult for us to understand who the God of love is. These distortions interfere with our ability to express our feelings to God and to trust him. This guide helps us to identify the distortions we have and to come to a new understanding of who God is. Six studies, 64 pages, 1152-4.

*Recovery from Family Dysfunctions.* Dysfunctional patterns of relating learned early in life affect all of our relationships. We trust God and others less than we wish. This guide offers healing from the pain of the past and acceptance into God's family. Six studies, 64 pages, 1151-6.

*Recovery from Loss.* Disappointment, unmet expectations, physical or emotional illness and death are all examples of losses that occur in our lives. Working through grief does not help us to forget what we have lost, but it does help us grow in understanding, compassion and courage in the midst of loss. This guide will show you how to receive the comfort God offers. Six studies, 64 pages, 1157-5.

*Recovery from Shame.* Shame is a social experience. Whatever its source, shame causes people to see themselves as unloveable, unworthy and irreparable. This guide will help you to reform your self-understanding in the light of God's unconditional acceptance. Six studies, 64 pages, 1153-2.